Don't Be a C*nt

A Modern Guide to Being Human

Don't Be a C*nt
Written by Jim McGee

ISBN: 979-8-9929960-1-2

First Edition

www.kr38iv.com/publishing

With a little help from my friends!

Foreword

Let's just get this out of the way: Americans underuse the word cunt.

The British know what's up. They don't toss it around lightly. It's reserved for the absolute worst— people who go out of their way to make life harder for everyone else. The selfish. The smug. The loud chewers. The "me first" crowd. The ones who ghost, honk, interrupt, and leave their dog's shit for someone else to step in.

This book is a modern take on *Rules of Civility & Decent Behavior*, the list of social commandments young George Washington copied down in the 1700s. Back then, it was all about not picking your teeth at the table or standing too close while someone's talking. It still holds up. But now, we've got
speakerphones in elevators, group texts with no boundaries, and people vaping in line at the DMV.

This isn't a guide for being fancy—it's a manual for being human. A reminder that being decent isn't complicated. It's about being aware of the people around you and doing your part to make the world suck a little less.

1

Mind your own goddamn business!
If no one asked, don't offer. If it's not your life, don't comment. It's really that simple.

2

Don't fake interest.
If you're texting, you're not listening.
Nodding while scrolling isn't presence—
it's disrespect.

3

Don't ask when someone's having kids.

Not your body. Not your business.

4

Don't assume everyone drinks.

Not everyone needs a reason.

5

Let people off the elevator before you get on.

You're not storming a castle.

6

Say "thank you" like you mean it.

Gratitude is free. Use it.

7

Apologize when you're wrong.
It's not weakness. It's decency.

8

Don't use "That's just how I am" as a pass.
If "how you are" is rude, change. Honesty without kindness is still just being a dick.

9

Don't try to convert people.
To your religion, diet, or crypto plan.

10

Don't shame people for what they can't afford.

You don't know their story.

11

Don't slam doors.
House, hotel, office, car — it doesn't matter. Close the door like a human being, not a gust of wind with unresolved trauma.
Walls shake, tempers rise, and no one's impressed.

12

Let people enjoy things.
Not everything needs your cynical take.

13

Don't give unsolicited advice.
Even if you're "just trying to help."

14

Don't make it a competition.
Let people share their story without
one-upping.

15

Watch where you're going.
Walking, driving—eyes up. If you're
moving, you're looking.
Not sideways. Not at your phone.
Look. Ahead.

16

Don't flirt with people at work.
It's not networking. It's just gross.

17

Learn people's names. And use them.
It matters more than you think.

18

Use your turn signal.
You're not mysterious. You're a hazard.

19

Don't tailgate.
We get it—you're in a hurry.
So were the 950,000 people
rear-ended last year.

20

Don't cut in line.
We all saw you. We're just too polite to call you out.

21

Be on time.
And if you're late, just say so. Skip the
excuses—we don't believe them anyway.

22

Don't park like you're the only one who matters.

Center it, genius. Your pickup truck is not a compact, no matter how tiny your self-esteem is.

23

Don't ride your bike like you're above the law.
You wanted to share the road—so stop treating red lights like suggestions.

24

Don't walk four-wide on a sidewalk.

Unless you're in a parade.

25

Don't block doorways.
Pick a side or move out of the way.

26

Hold the door for the person behind you.
It costs nothing.

27

Use someone's correct pronouns.
It's basic respect. Not politics.

28

**Don't take phone calls in
the elevator.**
You're in a tiny metal box. Don't trap us
with you.

29

Don't let your ringer blast in public.
If your phone makes more noise than a
toddler on Redbull, silence it like an adult.

30

Don't FaceTime without texting first.
It's not cute. It's intrusive.
Just send a quick message before
popping up uninvited on someone's
screen.
If it's an emergency, call.

31

Watch your mouth around children and the elderly.

It's not about censorship—it's about respect.

32

Your phone shouldn't make noise in public.

Music, Facetime, Speakerphone, videos, social media—on planes, buses, or in the office, that's what headphones are for. No one wants to hear your movie, Karen.

33

Don't leave voice notes longer than a minute.
This isn't a podcast.

34

Don't comment on someone's body. Ever.

It's not your business, even if you think it's a compliment.

35

**Don't blind everyone
with your phone.**
A screen on max brightness in a dark
room or filming with your flash on is
distracting and annoying.

36

Put your phone away at dinner.
You're not that important.

37

**Don't correct grammar
in casual texts.**

You're not an editor. You're annoying.

38

Don't ghost people.
Silence isn't closure. Be a grown-up.

39

RSVP and show up.

You're not a maybe. You're a yes or a no.

40

If you borrow it, return it better than you got it.

With thanks. And maybe snacks.

41

Don't humblebrag.
It's still bragging.
But now it's annoying too.

42

Don't brag about how busy you are.

It's not a flex. It's a cry for help.

43

Don't fake allergies to be dramatic.
You're not deathly allergic to cilantro.
You just don't like it.

44

**Don't bring strong scents
into shared spaces.**

Perfume, cologne, tuna—it's all too much.
Microwaving fish for lunch is terrorism.

45

Don't fake being an "empath" to excuse your behavior.

You're not feeling others—you're deflecting your own mess.

46

Don't overstay your welcome.
Read the room. Or the yawn.

47

Don't clap when the plane lands.
The pilot is not a magician.

48

Let people in front of you walk off the plane before you push forward.

It's not a race. We're all getting out.
In order.

49

Don't recline your seat unless it's time to sleep.
And if you have to, look first—and recline slowly.

50

The window seat decides if the window is open, and the middle seat gets both armrests.
That's the social contract of flying.
Don't like it?
Choose your seat accordingly.

51

Don't assume someone will swap seats with you on a plane.
Ask politely, and take no for an answer with grace.
The aisle, the legroom, or the window might matter more to them than it does to you.

52

Don't record people without permission.

You're not a journalist.
You're just annoying.

53

Don't share spoilers without a warning.

Some of us still enjoy surprises.

54

Clean up after yourself in public spaces.
Your barista isn't your maid.

55

Don't leave your dishes in the sink "to soak."
We all know what that means.

56

Put your shopping cart back.

It's not that hard. You're not that busy.

57

Tip your servers appropriately.
If you can't afford the tip,
you can't afford the meal.

And if you're not tipping the
housekeeper, the least you can
do is leave the room tidy.

58

**Don't tag people in
unflattering photos.**

Do you want war?

59

Don't fake laugh.
People can tell. It's worse than no laugh.

60

Don't interrupt.
Wait your turn. It's not hard.

61

Don't argue just to argue.
This isn't a debate club.
You're just exhausting.

62

Don't use "devil's advocate" as an excuse.

Seems like you just want to be a dick.

63

Don't talk politics at a first meeting.
Unless you like awkward silence.

64

If you're sick, stay home.
You're not "pushing through."
You're contagious.

65

Pick up after your dog.
Nobody should have to side-step
landmines just because you
 "forgot a bag."

66

Leash your dog.
It's not about how smart or friendly your dog is. It's about everyone else.
Get a leash- anything over 10 feet is a trip hazard.

67

Don't eavesdrop and then comment.

It's creepy. You weren't invited.

68

Use the crosswalk.
Just because you're on foot doesn't
mean laws don't apply to you.

69

**Don't hold up the crowd
for your photo.**
Take the pic and move out of the way.

70

Don't mansplain.
You're not helping. You're just annoying.

71

Don't touch people without asking.

Consent isn't just about sex.

72

Don't put your feet on public furniture.
This isn't your couch. It's disgusting.

73

Don't take your frustration out on customer service.
That worker didn't invent the policy—
and bullying someone who can't fight
back doesn't make you assertive,
it makes you an asshole.

74

Don't force small talk on trapped people.
Elevators, Ubers, Airplanes—
let them vibe.

75

Don't stand too close in line.
It's not a conga. Back up.

76

Don't fake a crisis to get attention.
Therapy is cheaper in the long run.

77

Don't shout, especially indoors.
Being loud doesn't make you right
—it just makes you aggressive.

78

Don't say "calm down."
It will never work.

79

Don't cheat at trivia night.
If you need Google to win bar bragging
rights, you already lost.

80

Don't shame people's hobbies.
Let them crochet in peace.

81

Don't send multi-text rants.
Write an email. Or better, don't.

82

**Don't stand over people
while they work.**

You're not supervising. You're just weird.

83

Don't swipe when someone shows you a photo on their phone.
You were shown one photo.
Swipe at your own risk.
Better yet, just don't.

84

Verify before you share.

"Some guy online said" is not a source.

85

Don't abuse ADA protections.
Faking a service animal or using mobility aids just because you're lazy disrespects people who actually need them.

86

Don't lie when "I don't know" would do.

Uninformed confidence isn't wisdom— it's how bad decisions start.

87

Don't trash shared spaces and say "they'll clean it."

You're not royalty. You're just rude.

88

**Don't act like rules don't
apply to you.**
They do. Even when no one's watching.

89

**Don't treat public restrooms
like a war zone.**

Flush. Wipe. Wash. Repeat.

90

Don't hover.
At the bar, at the table, at the copier.

91

**Don't cut people off when
they're speaking.**

You're not clairvoyant—you're just rude.

92

Don't confuse gossip with connection.
Talking about people behind their back
doesn't make you interesting—
it makes you disposable.

93

Don't chew with your mouth open.
You're a grown adult, not a pig at a trough. Close your mouth before we lose our appetite.

94

Give up your seat if someone needs it.

Use your eyes. Act like a human.

95

Help the helpless.
Kids, animals, strangers in a bad spot—
do the right thing. If someone needs
defending, speak up.

96

Don't correct people in public.
You're not smarter. You're just an ass.

97

Don't "reply all" unless it actually includes everyone.
Your whole team doesn't need your "Thanks!" email.

98

Ask before bringing your kids to adult spaces.
Not every event is family-friendly. Don't assume.

99

When you're staying in someone's home, act like it.

You're not at a hotel. Pick up your stuff, say thank you, and don't treat the coffee table like a laundry basket.

Don't be a cunt.
The golden rule, really.